D0470376

A R R A N G E D   B Y   J O H N   V A L E R I O

ISBN 0-7935-1658-7

© The Walt Disney Company

Hal Leonard Publishing Corporation
7777 West Bluemound Road P.O. Box 13819 Milwaukee, WI 53213

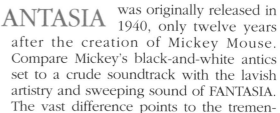

FANTASIA was originally released in 1940, only twelve years after the creation of Mickey Mouse. Compare Mickey's black-and-white antics set to a crude soundtrack with the lavish artistry and sweeping sound of FANTASIA.

The vast difference points to the tremendous advancement made by Walt and his staff. As Disney reminisced, "Although the Mickeys were successful, all of us wanted to do a type of picture that veered away from the out-and-out slapstick. That's the way the Silly Symphonies started. As musical backgrounds we used to record music from the classics rather than from something like 'Turkey in the Straw' or 'Frankie and Johnnie.' And the subject matter was always something appealing that would be in line with the music used."

Throughout the 1930s, Walt Disney made great strides with his series of Silly Symphony cartoons, but they were regarded as stepping stones toward his goal of animated features. SNOW WHITE AND THE SEVEN DWARFS, his first feature, had set a standard of excellence, and Disney realized that all his future films would have to equal or surpass it in quality.

In departing from the pattern of the Silly Symphonies, Disney decided to select a piece of music that already had a story to it. There was no argument when Paul Dukas' "The Sorcerer's Apprentice" was suggested. The music, telling the legend of the wayward apprentice who discovered he could not handle his mentor's powers, was ideal for trying out the new premise. As soon as the rights were obtained, Walt Disney began considering the use of a well-known conductor to add further prestige to the project. Leopold Stokowski, conductor of the Philadelphia Orchestra since 1912, recalled: "I first met Walt Disney in a restaurant. I was alone having dinner at a table near him, and he called across to me, 'Why don't we sit together?' Then he began to tell me how he was interested in Dukas' 'The Sorcerer's Apprentice' as a possible short, and did I like the music. I said I liked it very much and would be happy to cooperate with him." In follow-up discussions, Disney representatives discovered that Stokowski had some very interesting ideas about instrumental coloring, which would be perfect for an animation medium; they also discovered that he had experimented already with revolutionary methods of sound recording for the movies.

The Disney storymen and animators began work on the story late in 1937. An early decision cast the most popular "star" in the Disney Studio - Mickey Mouse - as the title character, a decision which at first was not especially popular with Mr. Stokowski, who had suggested the creation of a new and different Everyman character for the role. The artists were instructed to remember that the picture would "be made without dialogue and without sound effects, depending solely on pantomime and the descriptive music."

As the recording and the animation proceeded, the costs of the film mounted alarmingly fast. By the time "The Sorcerer's Apprentice" was finished in 1938, the cost was three to four times that of a normal Silly Symphony, and Disney came to realize he would never get his expenses back if the film was released as a short. Disney's thoughts turned to a full-length feature film. Production supervisor Ben Sharpsteen recalled, "Quality came first in Walt's opinion; box-office will follow quality. This was the birth of a new concept, a group of separate numbers - regardless of their running time - put together in a single presentation. It turned out to be a concert - something novel and of high quality."

Disney asked Stokowski to return to the Studio to help select the musical works to be included, and joining him as musical advisor was the noted music critic and composer, Deems Taylor. Walt Disney did not claim to be a musician himself. Nevertheless, Stokowski commented that Disney was a natural musician by instinct. While working on FANTASIA, Stokowski was constantly amazed at the reactions and impressions which Disney received from the music of the great masters. Together they studied hundreds of world-famous masterpieces, listening to recordings by the hour, arranging tentative programs and rearranging them, suggesting action which might be used to interpret the various pieces. Works were chosen which were very different in mood and tempo, with the premise that the orchestra would be presenting an evening's concert, interpreted on the screen by the artistry of Walt Disney and his staff.

As the elements comprising the program slowly fell into place, it was a unanimous decision to open the concert with Bach's "Toccata and Fugue in D Minor." Stokowski was known for rewriting many of Bach's keyboard works for orchestra, and his first performance of his new arrangement of this piece with the Philadelphia Orchestra had created a sensation, and added it forever to the symphonic repertoire.

The piece bore no title, beyond a purely descriptive one. It evoked no definite pictures, suggested no definite action, told no story. It was chosen because it gave the artists a chance to work with an abstract piece of music. As Walt Disney recalled, "The abstractions were no sudden idea. Rather they were something we had mused along for several years but we never had the chance to try, due to the fact that the type of pictures being made up to that time did not allow us to incorporate any of this type of material in them." One of Disney's early steps had been the hiring of German abstractionist filmmaker Oskar Fischinger to offer advice to his staff.

In "The Nutcracker Suite" segment, the Disney staff outdid themselves in finding revolutionary new ways of handling paints, pastels, and crayons, and in exploring new ways of manipulating the giant multiplane camera.

Tchaikovsky's music appealed to Disney, but he chose not to use the characters usually associated with it - the nutcracker himself is nowhere to be seen - but instead to conceive new characters from the world of nature. The first two movements of the suite have been omitted and the original order of the movements altered, but because of the form of the suite, no harm has been done.

Following the humorous relief of "The Sorcerer's Apprentice" in the program came the most modern piece, Stravinsky's "Rite of Spring." The audience at the first performance in Paris was so unfamiliar with the discordant sound and brutal rhythms that some listeners were outraged. Others were intensely excited, and the performance ended abruptly in a free-for-all riot. In recent years, "Rite of Spring" has come to be regarded by musicians and critics as a significant milestone in modern music. For years, since seeing the early "Gertie the Dinosaur" cartoons, Walt Disney had been intrigued by the power and savage character of prehistoric creatures. He decided to use "Rite of Spring" to depict science's conception of the beginnings of the universe and follow the progress of earth from a molten mass of brilliant gases down through the passing of the dinosaurs.

Beethoven wrote his Sixth Symphony, "The Pastoral," recalling an idyllic country visit. The Disney artists kept the same mood in their visualization, but transported the scene from one which would have been familiar to the composer to the beautiful slopes of Mount Olympus, traditional abode of the Greek gods. Taking the characters out of the realm of mythology and bringing them to fascinating life, the artists presented a frolic reminiscent of the Silly Symphonies.

Ponchielli, an important figure in modern Italian opera, wrote the well-known ballet music "Dance of the Hours" for his opera, *La Gioconda*. Since the music was so well-known, the Disney artists felt no qualms about using it for comic relief, and calling upon designs inspired by the German artist, Heinrich Kley, presented a wild parody of ballet, starring a dance troupe the likes of which had never been seen before. For their research, the artists spent hours studying animals at nearby zoos and going to ballets. Film was taken of ballerinas, led by the future Marge Champion, so the animators could more closely study the motions.

One of the farthest departures from anything done previously by Walt Disney is the segment based on Mussorgsky's "A Night on Bald Mountain." By interpreting the awesome power of the evil forces of Darkness and the ultimate triumph of Light, Walt Disney reasoned that this segment would make a fitting climax to the film, juxtaposed with the "Ave Maria" which follows. Disney and his artists agreed that the profane and sacred contrast set off these two numbers to such a degree that they should be blended into each other by a musical bridge, but "A Night on Bald Mountain" turned out to end on a calm note, the same musical note with which "Ave Maria" began, so no bridge was necessary. Schubert's song has English lyrics which were written especially for FANTASIA by

Rachel Field. The sequence featured a spectacular use of the multiplane camera.

From their earliest discussions, Walt Disney and Leopold Stokowski wanted to experiment with new projection and sound techniques. Disney's dream of wide-screen projecting, predating CinemaScope® by many years, proved economically unfeasible at the time, but work progressed on what would be the first use of a stereophonic sound system, to be called Fantasound. It featured multi-track recording, and a unique system of speakers, so that the sound would surround the audience. Theaters would have to be specially equipped at great expense, necessitating a limited road-show distribution.

A contest was held within the Disney Studio to select a title for the film, with over 2,000 entries submitted. Finally, FANTASIA was selected; it is a musical term with two meanings, both of which applied - a composition in which the composer strayed from accepted form, and a potpourri of familiar airs.

The completed FANTASIA premiered on November 13, 1940, at the Broadway Theater in New York. Hermine Rich Isaacs wrote in *Theater Arts:* "That night, audiences were confronted for the first time on any large scale with two major innovations: an ingenious partnership between fine music and animated film, and an immeasurably improved method of sound reproduction." *Time Magazine* devoted a front cover to FANTASIA, along with a three-page article. The article appeared not under Cinema, but under Music. Most criticism in the reviews centered upon the "Pastoral" and "Rite of Spring" segments. The original audiences and critics were confronted with pictures that were often diametrically opposed to conceptions which they had built up in their own minds when listening to the familiar musical scores. But today, FANTASIA has become such a classic of the American film that the Disney visualizations have become almost as familiar as the music.

Walt Disney mentioned in *Time* that he expected FANTASIA to run for years, "perhaps even after I am gone." It took until 1969 for FANTASIA to become profitable because of its original appeal to an audience, differing from the usual Disney audience, its early road-show distribution in only 14 cities, and the fact that most foreign markets were effectively cut off by World War II. But today, it is regarded as a genuine cinema classic, and audiences flock to see it. It has been in constant reissue in selected situations since 1969, with its popularity ever increasing.

FANTASIA was more than ahead of its time - it was revolutionary. Not only did it establish animation as the true art form that it is, but it introduced stereophonic sound to motion pictures and popularized classical music with moviegoing audiences. In celebration of FANTASIA'S 50th anniversary, Stokowski's original recordings have been cleaned and restored through digital and state-of-the-art analog technologies. This historically preserved soundtrack presents future generations of music lovers with the authentic sparkle of FANTASIA for all time.

David R. Smith
Walt Disney Archives

TOCCATA AND FUGUE IN D MINOR

JOHANN SEBASTIAN BACH

Adagio

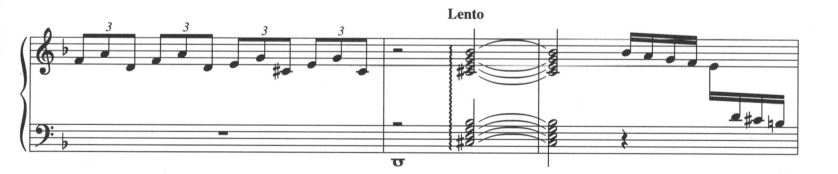

Prestissimo

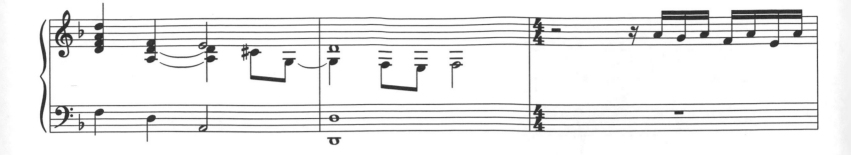

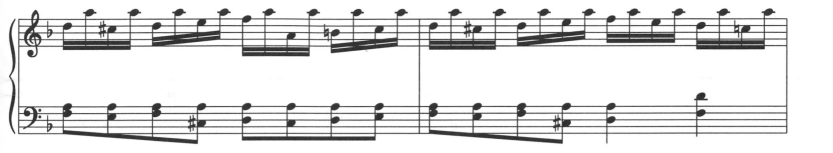

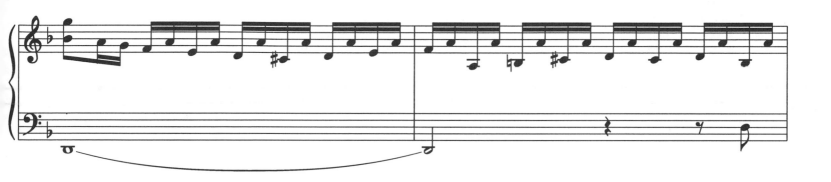

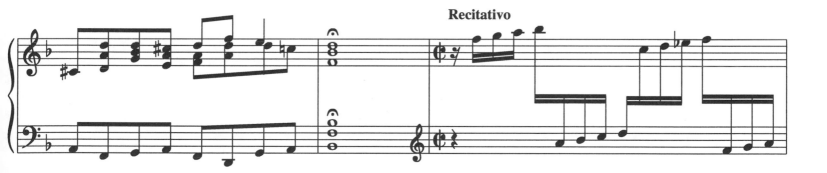

Recitativo

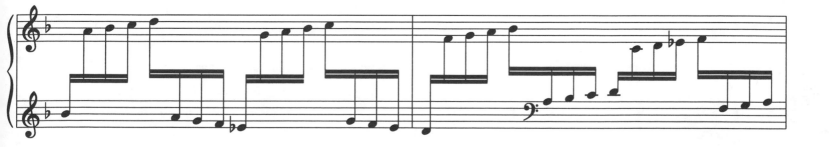

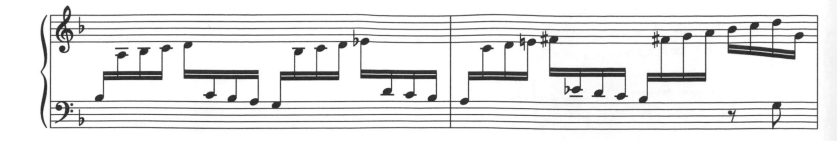

Adagissimo

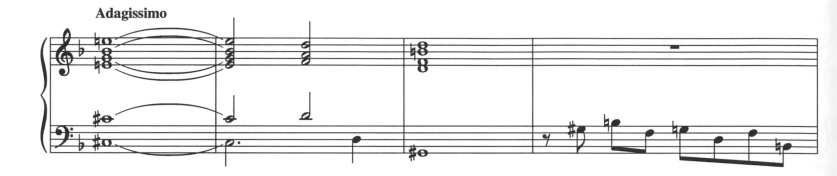

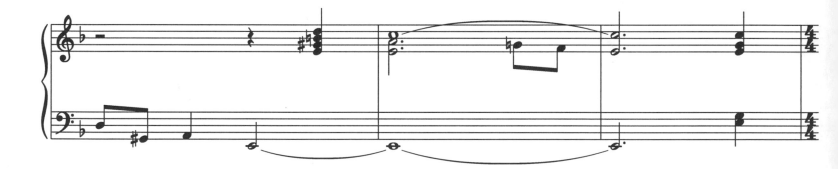

Vivace

Molto Adagio

DANCE OF THE SUGAR PLUM FAIRY

(From "THE NUTCRACKER SUITE")

PETER ILICH TCHAIKOVSKY

Andante non troppo

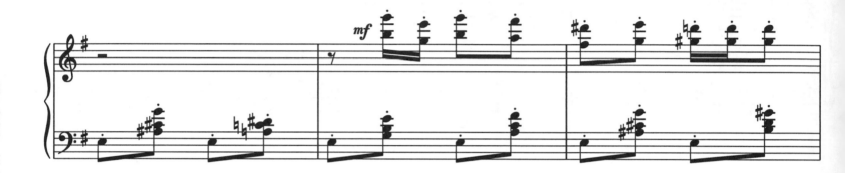

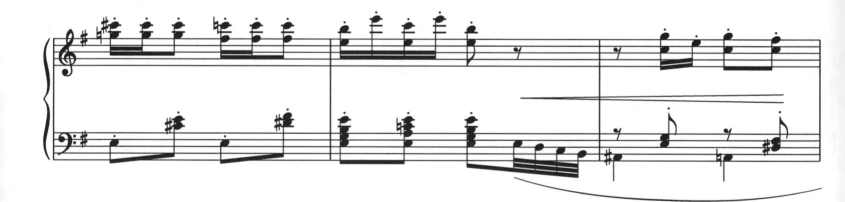

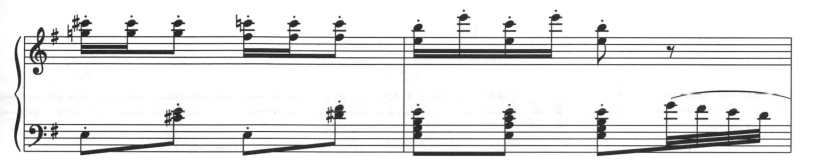

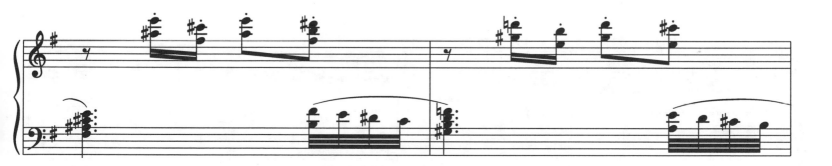

DANCE OF THE REED FLUTES

(From "THE NUTCRACKER SUITE")

PETER ILICH TCHAIKOVSKY

Moderato assai

ARABIAN DANCE
(From "THE NUTCRACKER SUITE")

Peter Ilich Tchaikovsky

Commodo

molto espress. e cantabile

CHINESE DANCE
(From "THE NUTCRACKER SUITE")

PETER ILICH TCHAIKOVSKY

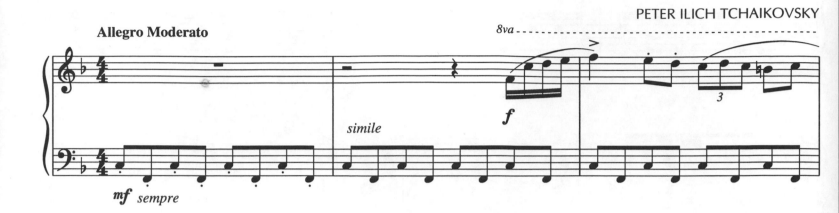

RUSSIAN DANCE

(From "THE NUTCRACKER SUITE")

PETER ILICH TCHAIKOVSKY

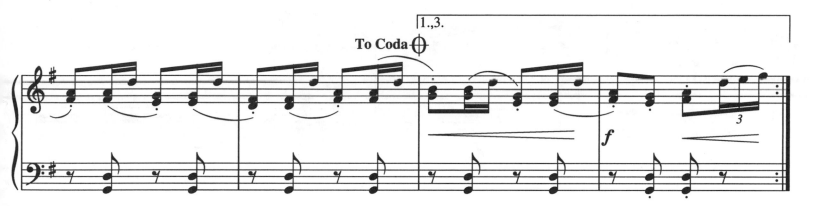

D.C. al Coda
(with repeat)

CODA

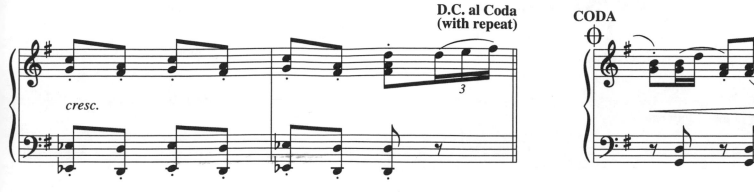

WALTZ OF THE FLOWERS

(From "THE NUTCRACKER SUITE")

PETER ILICH TCHAIKOVSKY

Valse Moderato

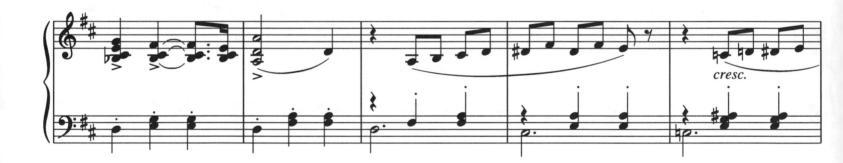

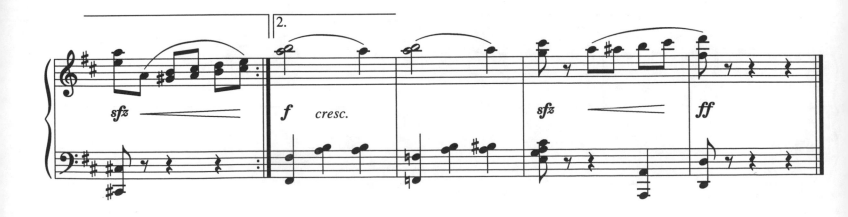

RITE OF SPRING

IGOR STRAVINSKY

Tempo Giusto

THE SORCERER'S APPRENTICE

PAUL DUKAS

poco cresc.

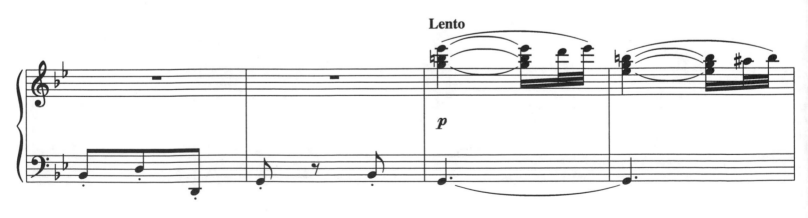

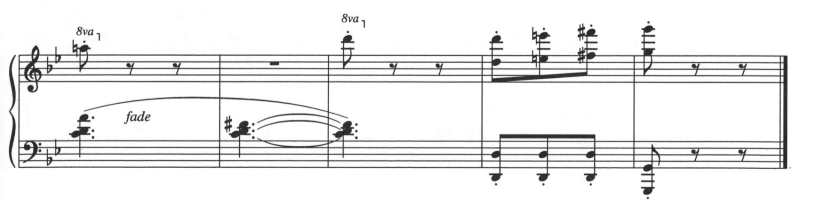

PASTORAL SYMPHONY
1st Movement Theme

LUDWIG VAN BEETHOVEN

Allegro ma non troppo

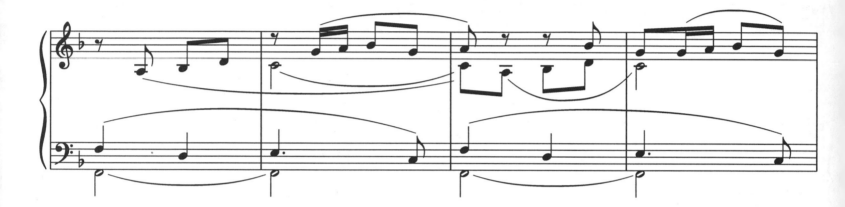

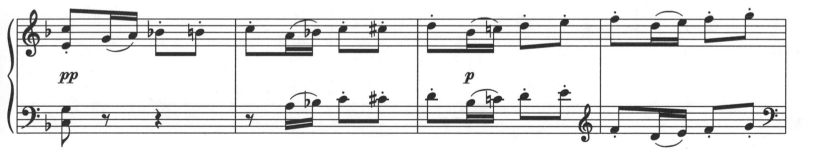

cresc.

f

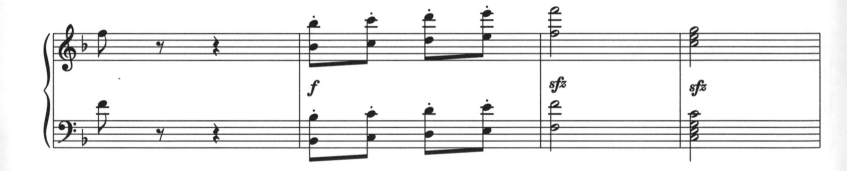

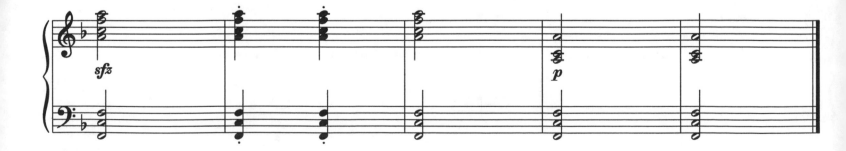

PASTORAL SYMPHONY
3rd Movement Theme

LUDWIG VAN BEETHOVEN

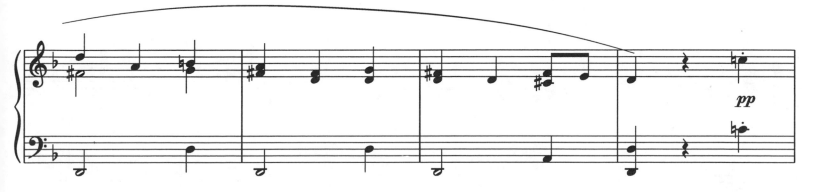

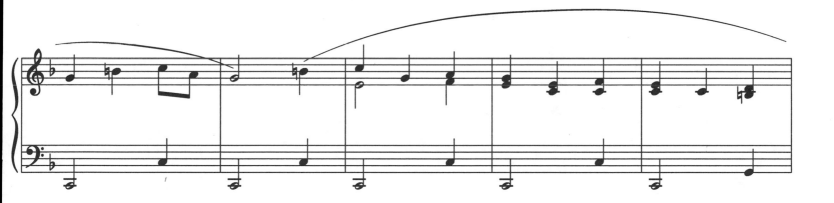

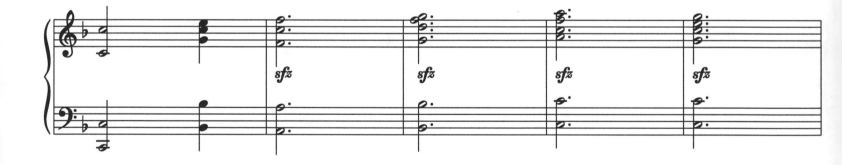

PASTORAL SYMPHONY
5th Movement Theme

LUDWIG VAN BEETHOVEN

Allegretto

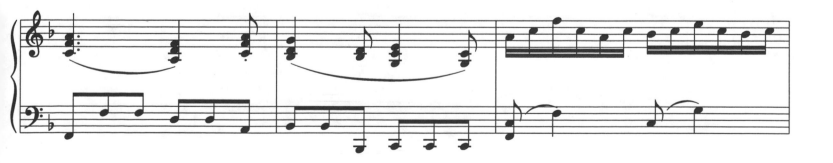

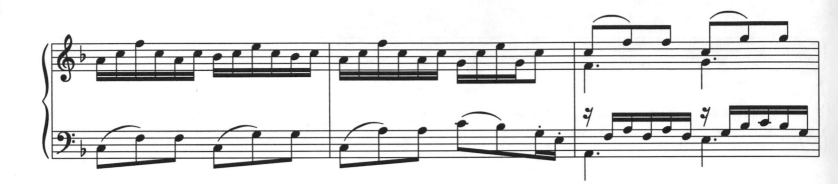

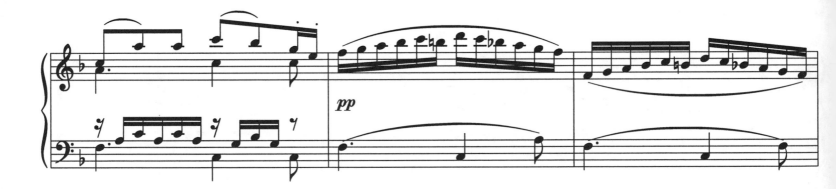

DANCE OF THE HOURS

AMILCARE PONCHIELLI

Moderato

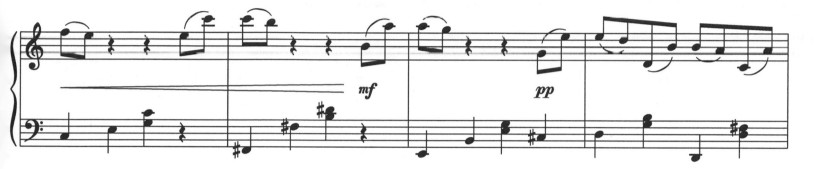

A NIGHT ON BALD MOUNTAIN

MODEST MUSSORGSKY

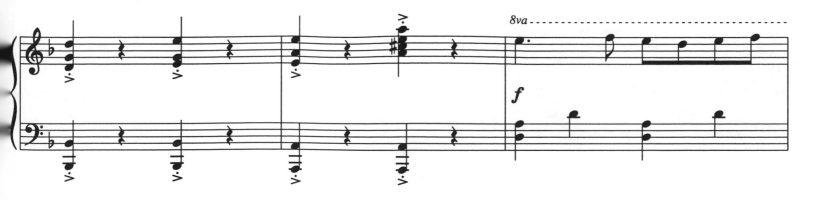

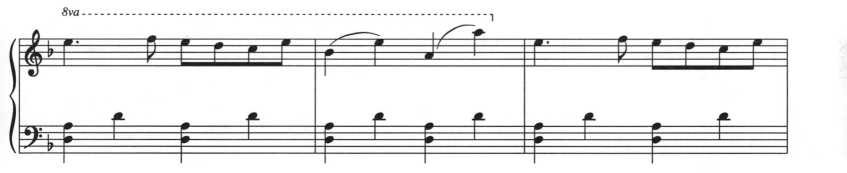

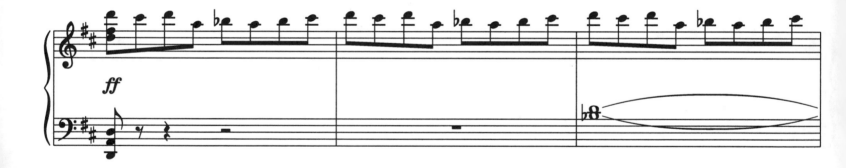

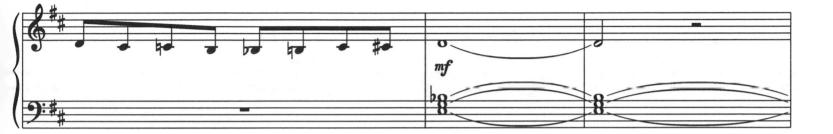

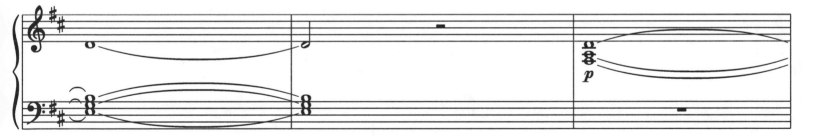

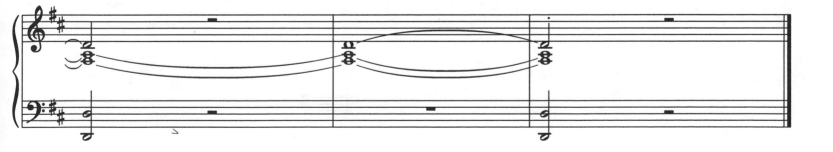

AVE MARIA

FRANZ SCHUBERT

Molto Lento

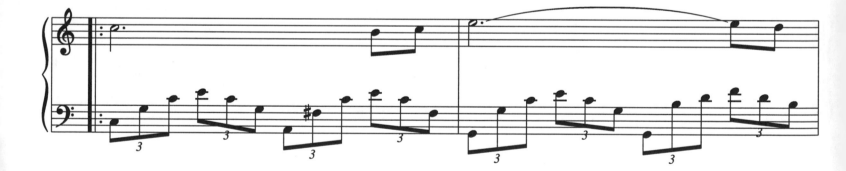